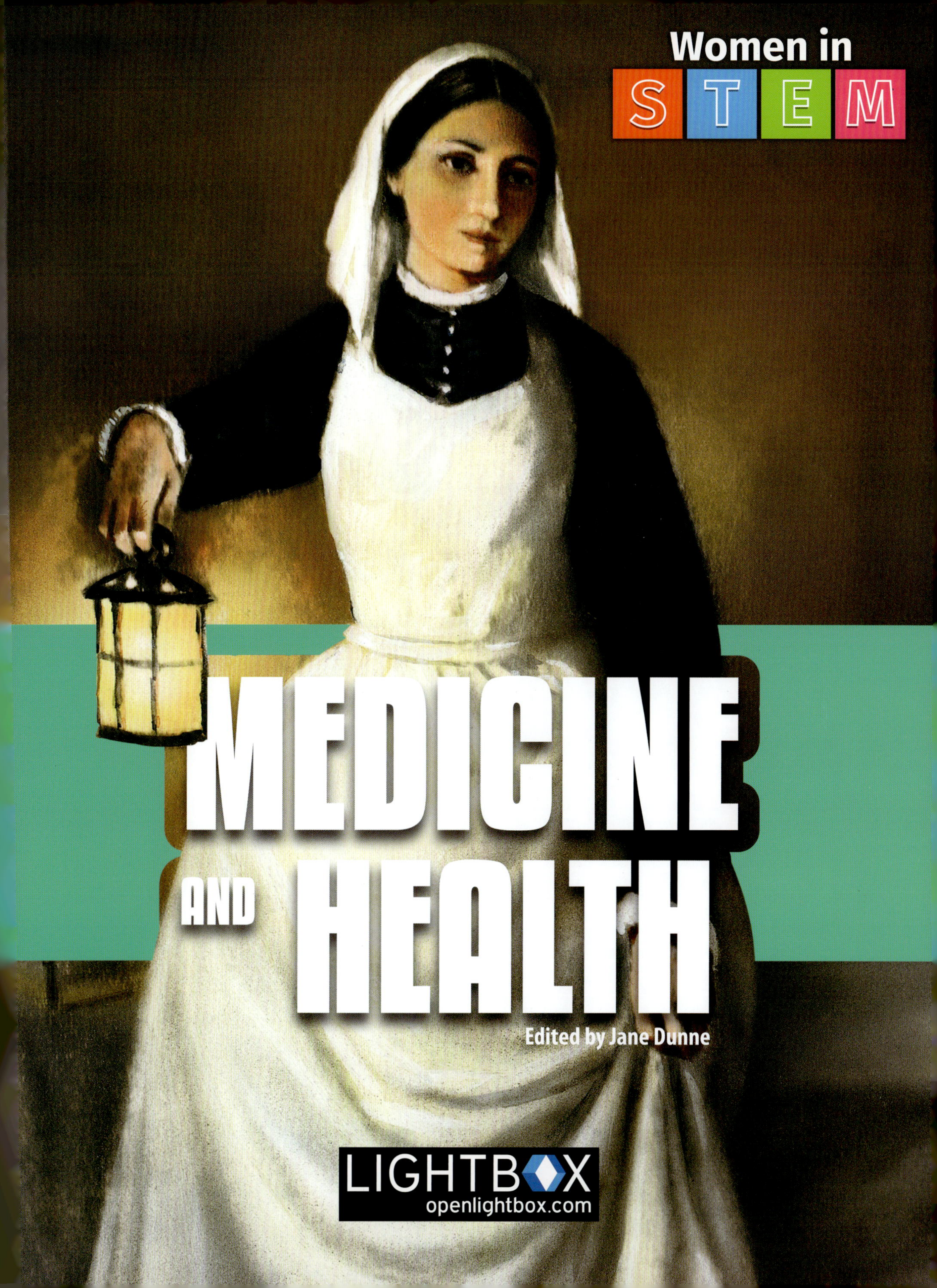

Women in STEM

MEDICINE AND HEALTH

Edited by Jane Dunne

LIGHTBOX
openlightbox.com

LIGHTBOX

Go to
www.openlightbox.com
and enter this book's
unique code.

ACCESS CODE

LBXH7357

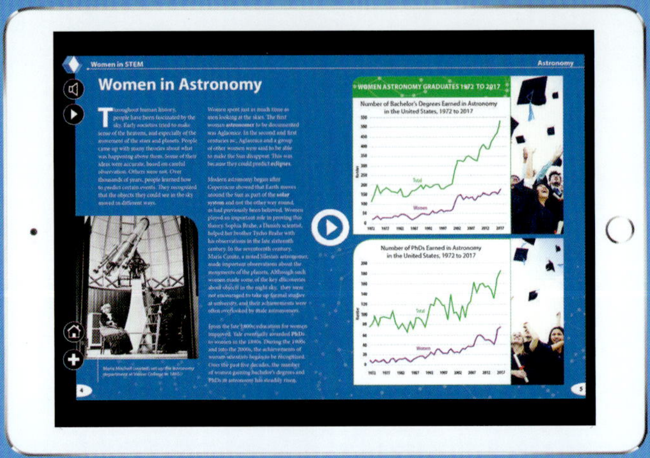

Lightbox is an all-inclusive digital solution for the teaching and learning of curriculum topics in an original, groundbreaking way. Lightbox is based on National Curriculum Standards.

STANDARD FEATURES OF LIGHTBOX

AUDIO High-quality narration using text-to-speech system

VIDEOS Embedded high-definition video clips

ACTIVITIES Printable PDFs that can be emailed and graded

WEBLINKS Curated links to external, child-safe resources

SLIDESHOWS Pictorial overviews of key concepts

TRANSPARENCIES Step-by-step layering of maps, diagrams, charts, and timelines

INTERACTIVE MAPS Interactive maps and aerial satellite imagery

QUIZZES Ten multiple choice questions that are automatically graded and emailed for teacher assessment

KEY WORDS Matching key concepts to their definitions

Women in STEM

MEDICINE AND HEALTH

CONTENTS

2 Lightbox Access Code
4 Women in Medicine and Health
6 Medicine and Health Worldwide
8 Florence Nightingale
10 Elizabeth Blackwell
12 Elizabeth Garrett Anderson
14 Melanie Klein
16 Rita Levi-Montalcini
18 Virginia Apgar
20 Timeline of Medicine and Health
22 Quiz
23 Key Words/Index
24 Log on to www.openlightbox.com

Women in Medicine and Health

Medicine is the **diagnosis**, treatment, and prevention of disease. The human body is complex, and people have always tried to understand how it works. Scientific discoveries have helped to cure people when they are sick. Other discoveries have helped to keep healthy people from getting sick.

Thousands of years ago, people knew very little about how the body worked. However, they used herbs and other natural substances as medicines. They also relied on spiritual healers. Women have always been involved in treating sick people. The first woman doctor to be written about in ancient Egypt was Merit-Ptah. In 2,700 BC, she was described as being the "Chief Physician." By about 2,000 BC, medicine was becoming a science. Doctors in Egypt, Rome, Greece, and China developed new theories about medicine and health, and began to explore human **anatomy**.

Long before women were allowed to train as doctors, they worked as nurses. During the Middle Ages in Europe, the sick were cared for in nunneries, where nuns lived as a religious community. In the 1400s and 1500s, only people who had trained at universities could become doctors in many countries. As most universities would not allow women to study, most doctors at the time were men.

Women have looked after other women in pregnancy for most of recorded history. Now, highly trained midwives have scanners to help them check on the health of the unborn child.

Nursing remained the major role for women in medicine. Many women specialized in looking after babies and the elderly. One exception to this was the Italian doctor, Anna Manzolini, who became a professor of anatomy in 1755. Important advances had been made in medicine by the 1800s. These included discoveries about how the blood is pumped around the body, and the role bacteria plays in the spread of diseases. Women, such as Florence Nightingale, realized the importance of **hygiene** and sanitation, and made great changes to the way the sick were cared for. Other women, such as Elizabeth Blackwell and Elizabeth Garrett Anderson, fought hard for women to be allowed to become doctors.

Today, the majority of medical students in the United States are women. They are studying in a range of specialty areas.

Hildegard of Bingen was a German abbess. In the 1100s, she wrote about plants that could help people who were sick.

Women have become prominent in the field of psychiatry, the diagnosis, prevention, and treatment of mental disorders. In the twenty-first century, the diagnosis of mental health issues is recognized as being vital for a patient's well-being.

FEMALE AND MALE SPECIALIZATIONS IN HEALTHCARE IN THE UNITED STATES

FEMALE DOCTORS are a majority in the following areas (FEMALES / MALES)

	Family medicine	Psychiatry	**Obstetrics**/Gynecology
Females	58 percent	57 percent	85 percent
Males	42 percent	43 percent	15 percent

MALE DOCTORS are a majority in the following areas

	Surgery	Emergency medicine	**Anesthesiology**	Radiology
Males	59 percent	62 percent	63 percent	73 percent
Females	41 percent	38 percent	37 percent	27 percent

Medicine and Health Worldwide

The ancient Greeks and Romans believed that four substances made up the human body. They thought that illness was caused by an imbalance between these four substances, or humors. Ancient Chinese doctors believed that energy, sometimes called Chi, flowed through the body. If the flow of energy was blocked, it caused sickness. Chinese doctors developed treatments such as **acupuncture** to unblock the energy.

In the 1600s, the English physician, William Harvey, discovered how blood circulated around the body. This was a great leap forward in medical science. By the 1900s, knowledge of anatomy, and discoveries such as **antibiotics** and anesthetics, were saving many lives. The improvement in medicine accelerated rapidly. Today, women take a leading role in treating the sick. Women are also leaders in all areas of scientific research, helping to find cures for diseases.

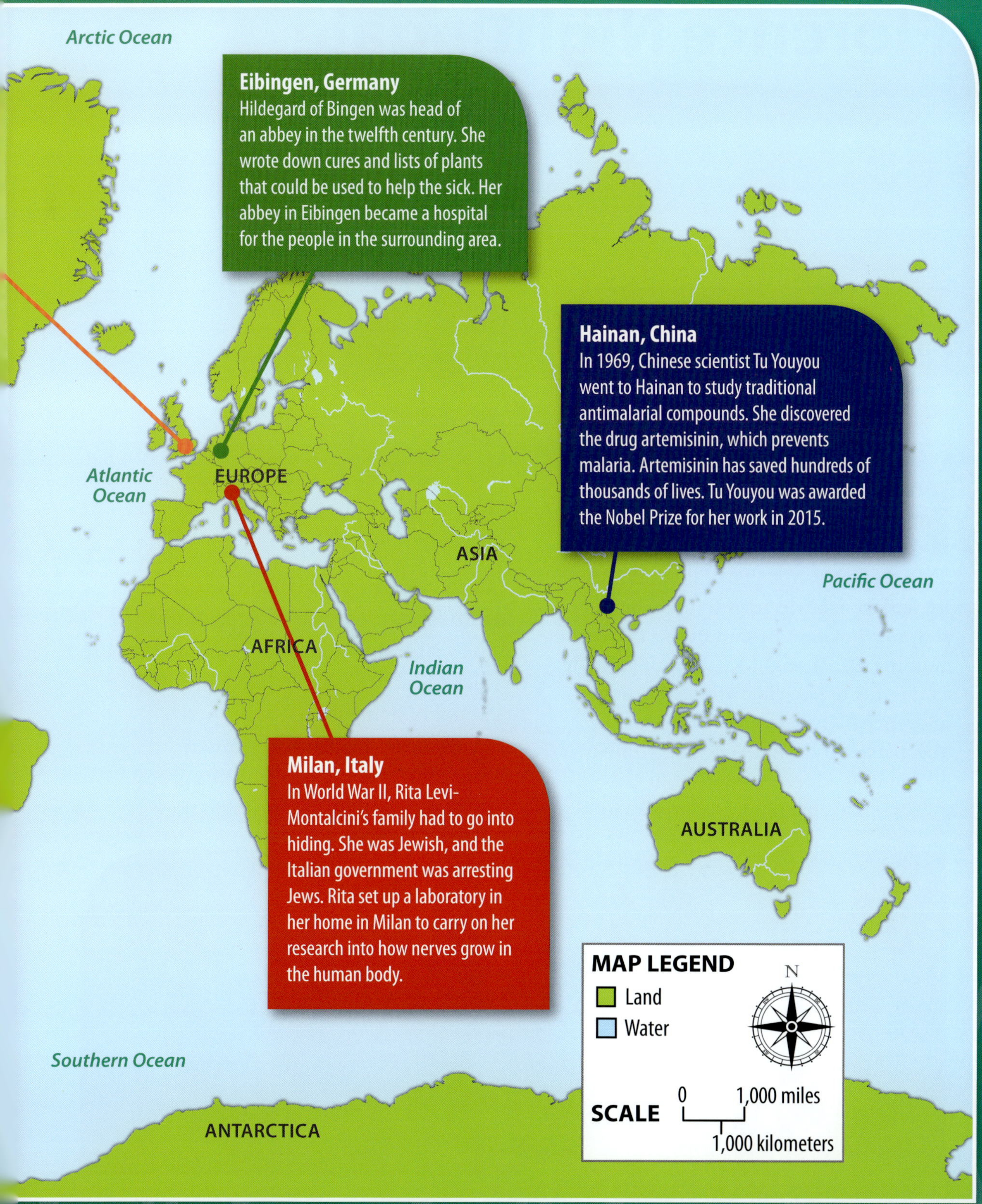

Eibingen, Germany

Hildegard of Bingen was head of an abbey in the twelfth century. She wrote down cures and lists of plants that could be used to help the sick. Her abbey in Eibingen became a hospital for the people in the surrounding area.

Hainan, China

In 1969, Chinese scientist Tu Youyou went to Hainan to study traditional antimalarial compounds. She discovered the drug artemisinin, which prevents malaria. Artemisinin has saved hundreds of thousands of lives. Tu Youyou was awarded the Nobel Prize for her work in 2015.

Milan, Italy

In World War II, Rita Levi-Montalcini's family had to go into hiding. She was Jewish, and the Italian government was arresting Jews. Rita set up a laboratory in her home in Milan to carry on her research into how nerves grow in the human body.

Florence Nightingale

Name: Florence Nightingale
Born: 1820, Florence, Italy
Died: 1910, London, Great Britain
Occupation: Nurse
Education: On-the-job training
Major discoveries and achievements: Pioneered modern nursing methods, set up first non-religious nursing school in the world
Major honors: Order of Merit, 1907; International Nurses Day is celebrated on her birthday, May 12.

Florence was educated at home by her wealthy father. He wanted her to have a good education. She studied French, German, Italian, and math. In 1850, Florence decided to become a nurse. In Great Britain in the 1800s, nursing was thought to be an unsuitable career for upper-class young women. Florence had to travel to Germany to receive her training. When she returned to London, Florence was put in charge of a woman's hospital. She proved to be not only a good nurse, but also an efficient manager.

In the 1850s, Great Britain was at war with Russia. The war took place on the Crimean Peninsula, on the coast of the Black Sea. It was reported that wounded were not being cared for properly. In 1854, the British government sent Florence to Crimea with a group of 38 nurses. The first hospital they

Florence was popular with wounded soldiers in Crimea. At night, she walked up and down the long hospital hallways. She carried an oil lamp, so the soldiers called her the "Lady with the Lamp."

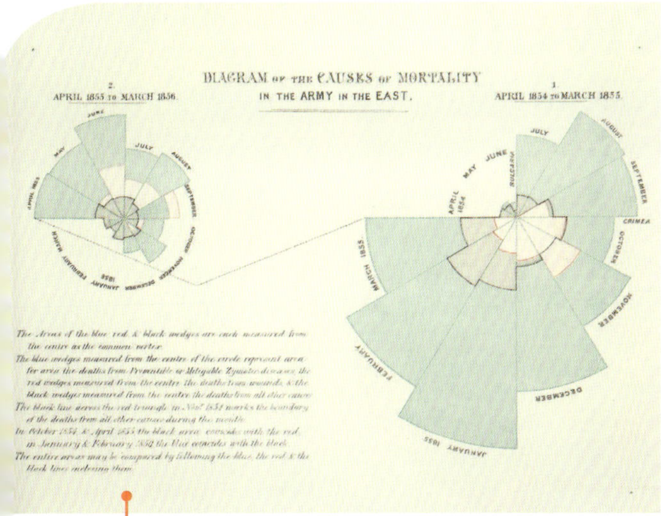

Florence's math education was useful in creating charts that showed the link between poor hygiene and disease.

visited was in Scutari, where more men were dying from disease than from their wounds. The hospital was filthy and infested with rats. Florence and her nurses cleaned the hospital with soap and water. They set up a laundry service, and organized clean drinking water. Death rates fell from 46 percent to less than 5 percent. Florence used **statistics** to explain how her methods worked.

When she returned to London, Florence had become a national hero. In 1859, she wrote *Notes on Nursing*, explaining how nursing standards could be improved. She also opened a training school for nurses. Florence spent the rest of her life improving nursing methods and standards of cleanliness and **nutrition** in hospitals.

MARY SEACOLE

Mary Seacole was also a nurse in the Crimean War. She was born in Jamaica in 1805, at a time when Jamaica was part of the British Empire. She nursed British soldiers suffering from tropical diseases in the West Indies, and tried to volunteer as a nurse during the Crimean War. Her application was refused. Mary was determined to help. She bought blankets, warm clothes, and healthy food for the soldiers, as well as her own medical supplies. In January 1855, she sailed to Crimea, where she met Florence Nightingale and set up the British Hotel on the peninsula. There, Mary cared for wounded soldiers waiting to be transported to Florence Nightingale's hospital in Scutari. By the end of the Crimean War in 1856, Mary had no money left, but the soldiers raised money for her so that she could pay her debts.

Mary was popular with the soldiers. They called her "Mother Seacole."

Elizabeth Blackwell

Name: Elizabeth Blackwell
Born: 1821, Bristol, Great Britain
Died: 1910, Hastings, Great Britain
Occupation: Physician
Education: Geneva Medical College, New York State
Major discoveries and achievements: First woman to achieve a medical degree in the United States, established a hospital for poor women and children
Major honors: The Elizabeth Blackwell Medal, awarded annually to a female physician, was established in her honor.

Elizabeth came from a wealthy family. Her father owned a sugar factory in Bristol. Elizabeth had a private tutor until fire destroyed the factory when she was 11 years old. After that, the family started a new life in the United States, first in New York, and then in Cincinnatti. While they were in Cincinnati, Elizabeth's father died, and Elizabeth and her sisters set up a small girls' school to earn some money. In 1842, Elizabeth moved to teach at a school in Kentucky. In Kentucky, she had a life-changing conversation with a friend who was ill. The friend said she wished she could be treated by a woman doctor. There were no women doctors in the United States at that time, so Elizabeth decided to become the first.

Finding a medical school to accept her was difficult. Elizabeth had saved enough money to pay fees, but 29 medical schools refused to allow her to attend because she was a woman. Finally, Geneva Medical School in New York gave her a place.

Elizabeth was admitted to Geneva Medical School in 1947. The male students had supported her and voted to offer her a place.

Elizabeth graduated from Geneva Medical School in 1849, at the top of her class. She was the first woman in the United States to earn a medical degree, but she did not want to stop there. Elizabeth wanted to qualify as a surgeon. She traveled to France to gain experience at a hospital in Paris. While treating a baby's eye infection, Elizabeth became infected in her left eye. She went blind in that eye, and with sight in only one eye, she had no hope of becoming a surgeon.

Elizabeth returned to New York in 1851, where she again found **prejudice** against women doctors. She could not get a job in any existing medical practice, so she started her own. In 1853, she opened a clinic for women in a poor neighborhood of New York. This quickly became successful, and with help from her sister and another woman doctor, it became the New York Infirmary for Indigent Women and Children. Indigent means poor, or needy. The hospital was staffed by women, and all illnesses were treated.

Elizabeth opened a medical college for women in New York in 1868, achieving a lifelong ambition. However, in 1869, she moved back to London after an argument with her sister over how their hospital should be run. Elizabeth practiced medicine in London and became a professor at the London School of Medicine. Her tireless efforts acted as an inspiration to all women wanting to gain medical degrees.

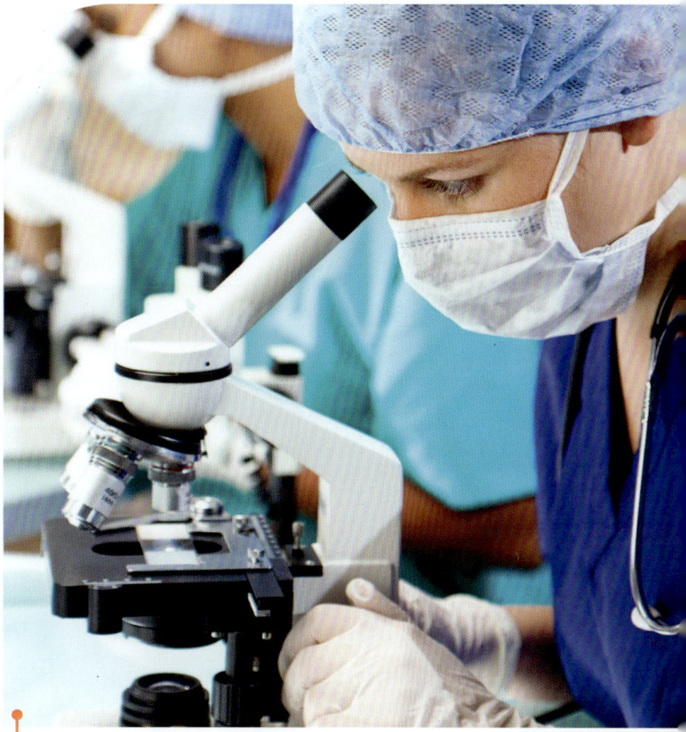

Elizabeth showed that women could be doctors. Since 1930, the number of women doctors and researchers in the United States has increased every decade.

From 1930 to 1970, **14,000 women** graduated from U.S. medical schools. This is **350 PER YEAR.**

From 1970 to 1980, **2,000 women** graduated from medical school per year in the United States.

In 2017, women formed **51 percent** of all medical students in the United States.

Elizabeth Garrett Anderson

Name: Elizabeth Garrett Anderson
Born: 1836, London, Great Britain
Died: 1917, Suffolk, Great Britain
Occupation: Physician
Education: Society of Apothecaries, University of Paris
Major discoveries and achievements: First woman to gain a medical qualification in Great Britain
Major honors: The Elizabeth Garrett Anderson Hospital in London was named after her.

Elizabeth was educated at home when she was young, and then went to a boarding school. The school did not teach much science, so she studied on her own after she left school. Elizabeth and her friends believed that women should have the same opportunities as men. Women should be allowed to study at university, and to vote in elections. One of Elizabeth's friends was Emily Davies, who later set up the first college for women at the University of Cambridge.

Elizabeth came to London in 1859 to meet Elizabeth Blackwell and attend lectures she was giving. Blackwell inspired Elizabeth to study medicine. Elizabeth began work as a nurse at Middlesex Hospital. She was allowed to watch operations, and to attend lectures, but her applications for medical school were turned down. Elizabeth was wealthy, so she hired a private tutor to teach her anatomy and **physiology**.

Elizabeth studied hard to qualify, and then practice, as a physician. She was determined that she would not let prejudice stop her medical career.

Elizabeth figured out that she would be allowed to practice medicine if she passed the exam of the Society of Apothecaries. An apothecary was originally someone who prepared and sold drugs. The society was not allowed to award medical degrees, but passing its exam would allow Elizabeth to practice medicine. Elizabeth passed the exam in 1865, and gained her medical license.

Despite her qualification, Elizabeth found it impossible to get a job at a hospital. Instead, she set up her own practice. Then, in 1866, she opened the St. Mary's **Dispensary** for Women and Children. In its first year, this dispensary treated 3,000 patients. It later became the New Hospital for Women. In 1870, Elizabeth finally received a degree in medicine from the Sorbonne University in Paris, France. Elizabeth then joined with Elizabeth Blackwell and other doctors to found the London School of Medicine for Women. This school offered degree courses in medicine to women.

In 1876, Elizabeth's efforts led to a new law in Great Britain that allowed British medical authorities to grant licenses to all qualified applicants, male or female. Even after she had retired from medicine, Elizabeth was a trailblazer. In 1908, she became the mayor of Aldeburgh, a small town in Great Britain. She was the first female mayor in England. She also supported her daughter, Louise, who was a leading campaigner for women's **suffrage**.

19 percent of surgeons in the United States are **women.**

1 percent of **surgery departments** in North America are headed by women.

In 1999, 7 percent of **Johns Hopkins surgeons** were women. Today, the figure is **27 percent.**

Elizabeth heard that the Sorbonne, in Paris, was prepared to accept female medical students. She learned French so that she could take the exams there.

Melanie Klein

Name: Melanie Klein
Born: 1882, Vienna, Austria-Hungary
Died: 1960, London, Great Britain
Occupation: Psychoanalyst
Education: Self-taught
Major discoveries and achievements: Showing the importance of play in child development. Devised Object Relations Theory, which looks at the development of a child's view of reality.

Melanie was the youngest child of a middle-class family. She wanted to study medicine, but she married when she was 21 years old. In the 1800s and early 1900s, women stopped working when they got married. Melanie gave up thoughts of a medical career, but regretted giving up the chance of becoming a doctor. She began to suffer from depression.

In 1910, Melanie, her husband, and her three children moved to Budapest. She went to see psychoanalyst Sandor Ferenczi about her depression. Ferenczi was a follower of Sigmund Freud. Freud had developed psychoanalysis, which was a method of treating people who had mental problems by talking to them and analyzing their thoughts. Melanie had read some of Freud's writings and became interested in psychoanalysis. Ferenczi was particularly interested in mental problems in children, and Melanie became fascinated by this, too. Melanie began to watch the way children played so that she could identify their anxieties and unspoken feelings. She published a paper about children's play in 1919.

Melanie's pioneering work continues to influence child psychology today.

In 1921, Melanie moved to Berlin, where she found some psychoanalysts were hostile to her ideas. In 1926, she moved to Great Britain, where she worked until her death.

Melanie's research was highly influential. She used aids, such as toys, to examine the way children think. Freud thought that dreams revealed the true personality of an adult, and Melanie believed that play could do the same for children. She showed that parents play a vital role in a child's view of the world. Her theories emphasized that a child's relationship with its mother shapes how a person later relates to situations and to other people.

Young children cannot answer questions about feelings in the same way an adult can. Melanie developed the idea of play therapy, where children express themselves through actions.

MELANIE KLEIN AND ANNA FREUD

Melanie and Sigmund Freud's daughter Anna were two of the most important women in the development of psychiatry in the 1940s. They both suffered from depression, both had bad relationships with their mothers, and both had strong ideas on how psychoanalysis could be used to understand child development. Their views clashed over the treatment of children, however. Anna was opposed to Melanie's view that watching children at play was the best way of gaining information. Melanie wanted to try different methods, and rejected many of Sigmund Freud's theories. This led to conflict in the world of psychoanalysis. In Great Britain, there was an agreement that both "Freudian" and "Kleinian" schools of thought should be allowed to follow their own paths, while remaining part of the Psychoanalytic Society.

Anna Freud believed that Melanie was moving away from the ideas that her father, Sigmund Freud, had developed.

Rita Levi-Montalcini

Name: Rita Levi-Montalcini
Born: 1909, Turin, Italy
Died: 2012, Rome, Italy
Occupation: Neurobiologist
Education: University of Turin
Major discoveries and achievements: Discovery of nerve growth factor (NGF)
Major honors: Nobel Prize in Physiology or Medicine, 1986; National Medal of Science, 1987; appointed Senator for Life in Italy, 2001

Rita's father and mother wanted Rita and her twin sister, Paola, to follow a traditional path in life. At the time, that meant getting married, and not going to college or having a career. As a teenager, Rita wanted to be a writer. However, after being deeply affected by the death of a childhood friend from cancer, she told her father that she had decided to become a doctor.

In the 1950s, Rita's experiments with mice led to the discovery of how nerves grow. Today, scientists using Rita's discovery hope to develop treatments for brain tumors and other diseases.

Rita managed to persuade her parents that she should be allowed to study medicine. She went to the University of Turin and graduated in 1936. She then stayed on at the university and did medical research into how the **nervous system** works.

Rita's medical career was interrupted by politics in 1938. The ruler of Italy was Benito Mussolini. His government ruled that Jewish people were not allowed to work in universities, and not allowed to study medicine. Rita was Jewish, so she lost her job. She created her own laboratory at home and carried on with her research into the nerve fibers of chicken **embryos**. When Italy entered World War II in 1940, Rita and her family had to go into hiding. She continued her research when the war ended in 1945.

In 1947, Rita was invited to Washington University in St. Louis. While there, she made a breakthrough in 1952, when she put a tumor from a mouse into a chick embryo. Rita noticed that the tumor had caused the nerves in the chick embryo to grow rapidly. She realized that the tumour must be releasing a substance that encouraged **nerve cell** growth. Working with a colleague, Stanley Cohen, she was able to find the substance and analyze it. They called the substance nerve growth factor (NGF). NFG is important because it lets nerve cells communicate with each other and helps them to grow. Other scientists were able to use this discovery to greatly extend their understanding of how the brain and nervous system works. This is one of the most complex areas of modern medicine, and Rita's work helped to make later medical breakthroughs possible.

NERVE GROWTH FACTOR (NGF)

Nerve growth factor (NGF) may eventually lead to cures for many conditions affecting the brain and the nervous system. Rita regularly gave herself NGF eye drops and claimed that her brain became more active as a result. She also lived to be 103. NGF has been shown to help wounds heal more quickly. It also helps to suppress the appetite. This makes NGF a potentially useful treatment for obesity in the future.

The most significant use of NGF, however, may be in the treatment of Alzheimer's disease. NGF helps in the creation of new brain cells and fibers in Alzheimer's sufferers. In experiments with rats, NGF has been used to restore memory that had been damaged, but there is still much research to be done.

NGF may one day reverse the growths that cause Alzheimer's disease.

Virginia Apgar

Name: Virginia Apgar
Born: 1909, Westfield, New Jersey
Died: 1974, Manhattan, New York
Occupation: Physician and anesthesiologist
Education: Mount Holyoke College, Columbia University
Major discoveries and achievements: Invention of the Apgar Score
Major honors: Elizabeth Blackwell Award, from the American Women's Medical Association, 1966; Alumni Gold Medal for Distinguished Achievement, Columbia University College of Physicians and Surgeons, 1973

Virginia was full of energy as a child. She was interested in science from an early age, and by the time she went to high school, she knew she wanted to be a doctor. At Mount Holyoke, she majored in zoology. Virginia then went to Columbia, where she became one of only nine women in a class of 90 students taking a medical degree.

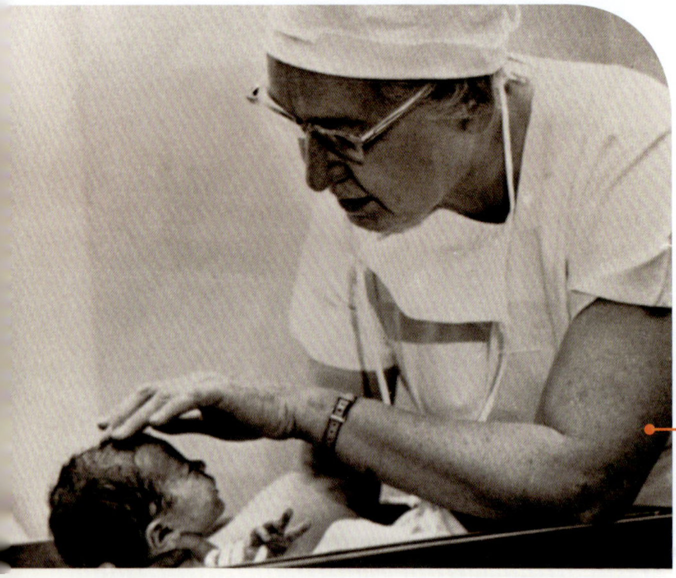

Virginia originally wanted to train as a surgeon, but she became interested in anesthesiology, which was a newly developing area of medicine. Anesthesiologists were trained to give patients the right drugs to stop them from feeling pain during and after an operation. As more drugs were becoming available, and more complex operations were being carried out, this branch of medicine required specialist training.

Virginia was among the first doctors to be trained in anesthesia. After her studies, she set up the first anesthesia department at the Columbia University hospital. She recruited and trained medical students, organized research projects, and supervised staff during operations.

Virginia worked at the Sloane Hospital for Women in the early 1950s. During this period, she was also a professor at Columbia University College of Physicians and Surgeons.

Some Apgar Score tables label the sections based on Virginia's surname. The sections are Appearance, Pulse, Grimace, Activity, Respiration.

In the late 1940s and early 1950s, Virginia worked in obstetrics. The number of babies dying in their early years in the United States was falling in the 1950s, but the number of babies dying within 24 hours of birth was still high.

Virginia's research showed that lack of oxygen was a major cause of death in babies. She developed a scoring system that doctors could use to help assess a newborn baby's health quickly. This system is known as the Apgar Score. There are five parts in Virginia's system, each part having a score of 0, 1, or 2. The maximum score is 10 for a healthy baby, but this is rare. If a baby scores under 3 points on the test, doctors need to take emergency action. Most hospitals carry out the test twice, at one minute and five minutes after birth.

In the mid-1960s, an outbreak of rubella, sometimes called German measles, caused thousands of infant deaths in the United States. Virginia helped to introduce a successful vaccination program for pregnant women, to stop unborn babies catching the disease. She also introduced the use of Rh testing on pregnant women. This identifies harmful **antibodies** in the blood that might be passed on to the unborn child. This test is still used today.

APGAR Test Scoring

	Score 0	Score 1	Score 2
Appearance	Blue all over	Blue only at extremities	No Blue coloration
Pulse	No pulse	<100 beats/min	>100 beats/min
Grimace	No response to simulation	Grimace or feeble cry when stimulated	Sneezing, coughing or pulling away when stimulated
Activity	No movement	Some movement	Active movement
Respiration	No breathing	Weak, slow or irregular breathing	Strong cry

In 2017, **60 percent** of doctors in the United States under the age of 35 were women.

In the mid-1960s, there were **12.5 million** cases of rubella in the United States. In 2004, there were 0.

In 2016, **80 percent** of U.S. master's degrees in **health sciences** were awarded to women.

Timeline of Medicine and Health

Long before they were allowed to train as doctors, women worked as nurses and healers. They used herbs and other natural remedies, passing down their knowledge from one generation to another. Then, from the 1800s, women in Europe and North America began training as medics and practicing as doctors. Many women have since played a major role in the advancement of medicine.

300 AD | 1200 | 1700 | 1800 | 1850

300 AD
Metadora writes a book in Greek about women's illnesses.

1165
Hildegard of Bingen founds a nunnery that acts as a hospital for local people.

1755
Anna Morandi Manzolini becomes professor of anatomy at Italy's University of Bologna.

1849
Elizabeth Blackwell becomes the first woman to graduate with a medical degree in the United States.

1854
Florence Nightingale organizes better sanitation in hospitals during the Crimean War.

The technology available to twenty-first century doctors would astonish early medical pioneers such as Elizabeth Blackwell. Thanks to the efforts of women throughout history, there are now more women medics than ever before.

1900 1950 1980 2000 2018

1919
Melanie Klein publishes her first paper on analyzing children at play.

1947
Rita Levi-Montalcini is invited to go to the United States to continue her studies of nerve growth in embryos.

1953
Virginia Apgar devises the Apgar Score to test the health of newborn babies.

1988
While researching in Germany, Patricia Bath invents the Laserphaco Probe, used in eye surgery.

2018
Women make up 53 percent of entrants for medical degrees at Johns Hopkins University School of Medicine in Baltimore.

Quiz

1 Where was Merit-Ptah called the "Chief Physician?"

2 What is the science of psychology?

3 What branch of medicine uses midwives?

4 Which war made Florence Nightingale a national hero?

5 Where did Elizabeth Blackwell eventually gain her medical degree?

6 Who took the exam of the Society of Apothecaries in order to practice medicine?

7 How did Melanie Klein use toys to explore the feelings of children?

8 What animals was Rita Levi-Montalcini studying when she made her breakthrough discovery?

9 What branch of medicine did Virginia Apgar first specialize in?

10 What is the maximum number achievable on the Apgar Score?

ANSWERS

1. Ancient Egypt **2.** The study of the mind and behavior **3.** Pregnancy and childbirth
4. The Crimean War **5.** Geneva Medical School **6.** Elizabeth Garrett Anderson
7. She observed how they played with toys to analyze their thoughts. **8.** Mice and chicks
9. Anesthesiology **10.** 10

Key Words

acupuncture: an ancient type of medicine that uses fine needles inserted into the skin at specific points to treat patients

anatomy: the study of the structure of the body

anesthesiology: the branch of medicine dealing with anesthetics, drugs that cause a loss of sensation, so that patients cannot feel pain

antibiotics: medicines that kill harmful bacteria

antibodies: substances in the blood that combine chemically with other substances for good or harmful effect

diagnosis: the identification of an illness from its symptoms

dispensary: a clinic that prepares and provides medicines

embyros: animals in their earliest stages of development, before birth

hygiene: practices that prevent disease, such as keeping clean

nerve cell: a type of cell that sends and receives messages

nervous system: the system in the body that responds to stimuli. The brain, spinal cord, and nerves make up the system.

neurobiologist: a scientist who deals with the health of the body's nervous system

nutrition: the provision of food necessary for health and growth

obstetrics: the branch of medicine dealing with pregnancy, childbirth, and the early period of a child's life

physiology: the branch of biology dealing with the function of body parts

prejudice: hatred or unfair treatment toward a person or group of people without cause

psychoanalyst: someone who treats mental problems by exploring a person's unconscious mental processes

statistics: the collection and analysis of numerical data

suffrage: the right to vote, particularly used about women's rights to vote

Index

Anderson, Elizabeth Garrett 5, 6, 12, 13, 22
antibiotics 6, 23
Apgar Score 18, 19, 21, 22
Apgar, Virginia 18, 19, 21, 22

Blackwell, Elizabeth 5, 10, 11, 12, 13, 18, 20, 21, 22

Cohen, Stanley 17
Crimean War 8, 9, 20, 22

Davies, Emily 12
doctors 4, 5, 6, 10, 11, 13, 18, 19, 20, 21

Freud, Anna 15
Freud, Sigmund 14, 15

Harvey, William 6

Klein, Melanie 14, 15, 21, 22

Levi-Montalcini, Rita 16, 17, 21, 22
London School of Medicine for Women 6, 13

medical degrees 11, 13, 21

nerve growth factor (NGF) 17
neurobiologists 16, 23
Nightingale, Florence 5, 8, 9, 20, 22
nurses 4, 8, 9, 20

object relations theory 14

play therapy 14, 15
psychoanalysts 15

Seacole, Mary 9
spiritual healers 4
surgeons 13, 18

tumors 16, 17

voting rights 13

World War II 17

LIGHTBOX

SUPPLEMENTARY RESOURCES

Click on the plus icon found in the bottom left corner of each spread to open additional teacher resources.

- Download and print the book's quizzes and activities
- Access curriculum correlations
- Explore additional web applications that enhance the Lightbox experience

LIGHTBOX DIGITAL TITLES
Packed full of integrated media

VIDEOS

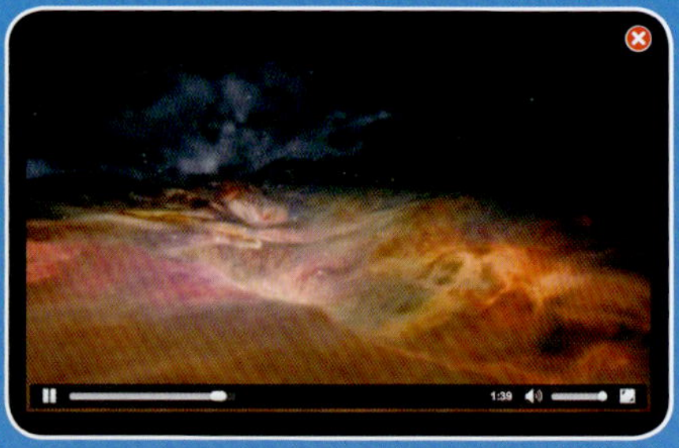

INTERACTIVE MAPS

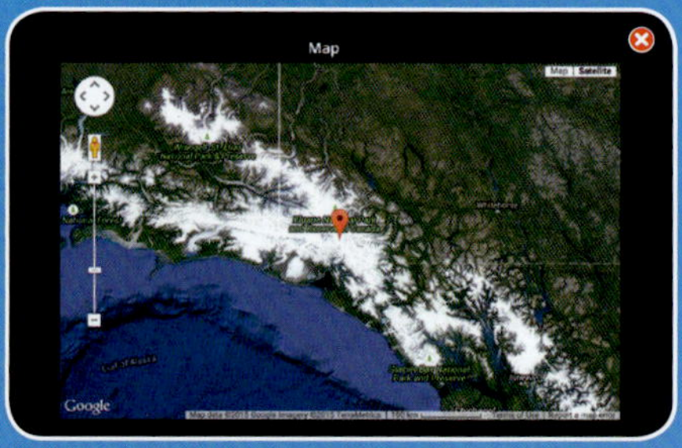

WEBLINKS

SLIDESHOWS

QUIZZES

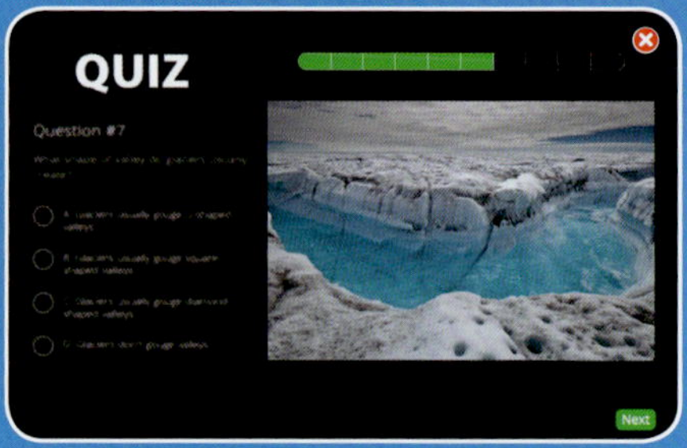

OPTIMIZED FOR

- ✓ TABLETS
- ✓ WHITEBOARDS
- ✓ COMPUTERS
- ✓ AND MUCH MORE!

Published by Smartbook Media Inc.
350 5th Avenue, 59th Floor New York, NY 10118
Website: www.openlightbox.com

Project Coordinator: Heather Kissock
Art Director: Terry Paulhus

Library of Congress Control Number: 2019905715

ISBN 978-1-5105-4434-5 (hardcover)
ISBN 978-1-5105-4435-2 (multi-user eBook)

Printed in Guangzhou, China
1 2 3 4 5 6 7 8 9 0 23 22 21 20 19

072019
311218

Photo Credits

Every reasonable effort has been made to trace ownership and to obtain permission to reprint copyright material. The publisher would be pleased to have any errors or omissions brought to its attention so that they may be corrected in subsequent printings.

The publisher acknowledges Getty Images, Alamy, Wikimedia, Dreamstime, and Shutterstock as its primary image suppliers for this title.